COME CLOSER, ROGER, THERE'S A MOSQUITO ON YOUR NOSE

Other FoxTrot Books by Bill Amend
FoxTrot
Pass the Loot
Black Bart Says Draw
Eight Yards, Down and Out
Bury My Heart at Fun-Fun Mountain
Say Hello to Cactus Flats
May the Force Be With Us, Please
Take Us to Your Mall
The Return of the Lone Iguana
At Least This Place Sells T-Shirts

Anthologies
FoxTrot: The Works
FoxTrot *en masse*
Enormously FoxTrot
Wildly FoxTrot
FoxTrot Beyond a Doubt

COME CLOSER, ROGER, THERE'S A MOSQUITO ON YOUR NOSE

A FoxTrot Collection by Bill Amend

Andrews McMeel Publishing

Kansas City

FoxTrot is distributed internationally by Universal Press Syndicate.

Visit *FoxTrot* on the World Wide Web at www.foxtrot.com

Information about Andrews McMeel Publishing can be found at www.andrewsmcmeel.com

ISBN: 0-8362-3656-4

Library of Congress Catalog Card Number: 97-71626

5

9

11

13

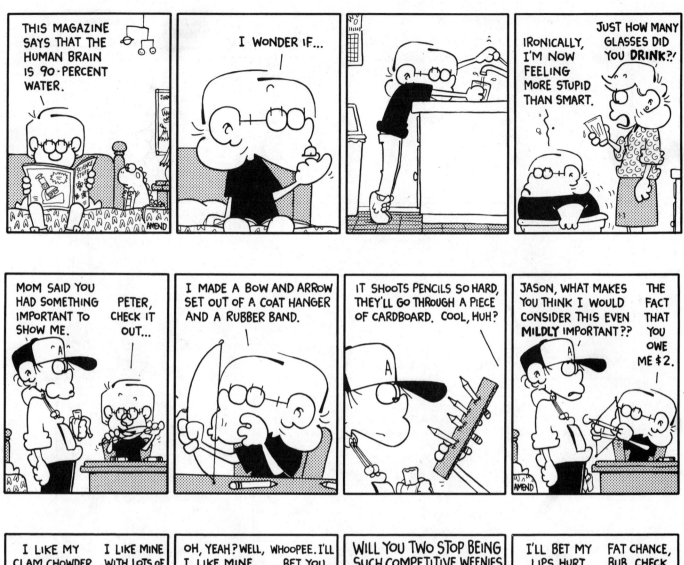

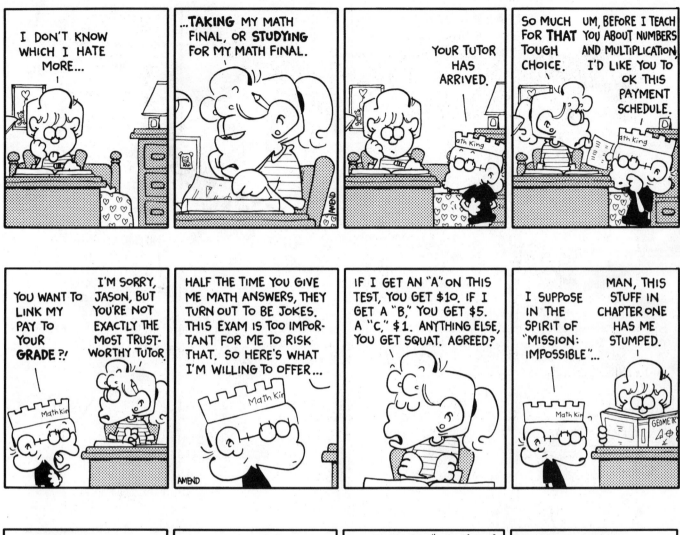

20

21

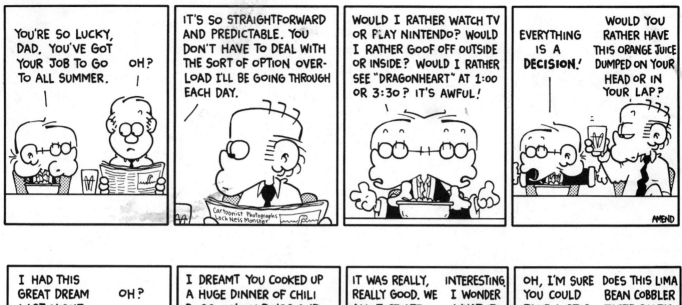

31

33

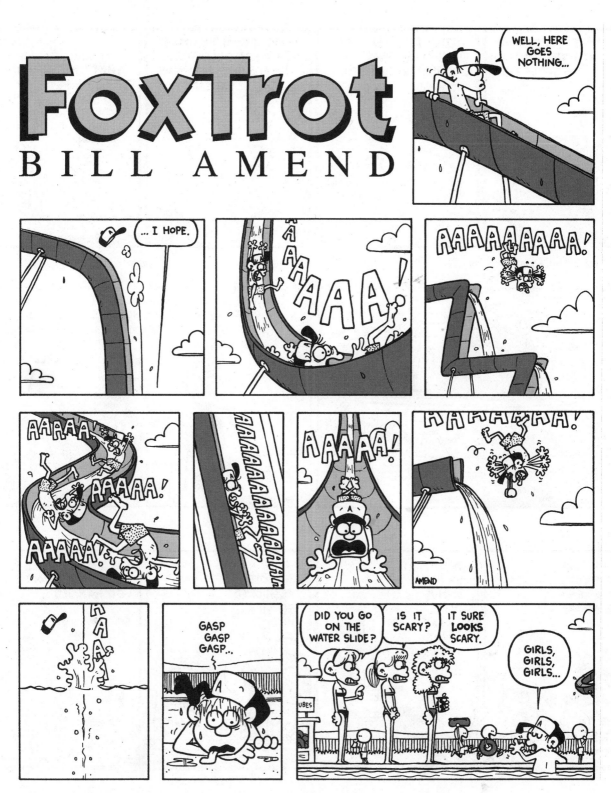

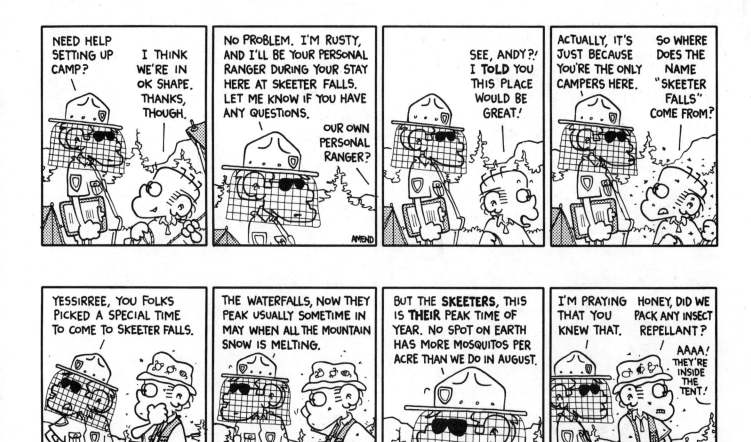

45

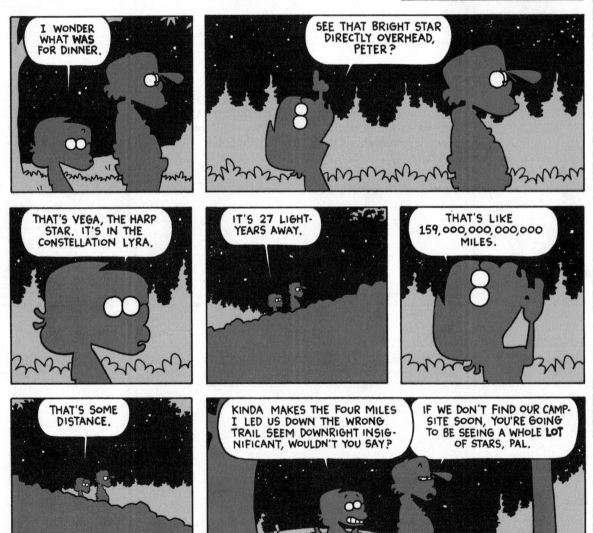

47

52

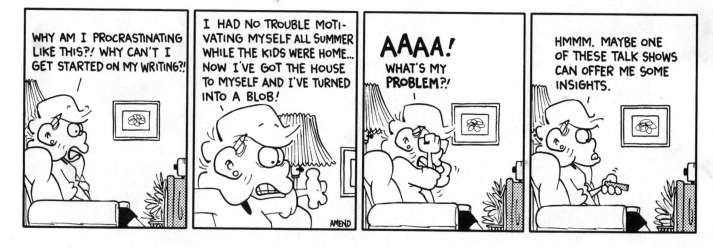

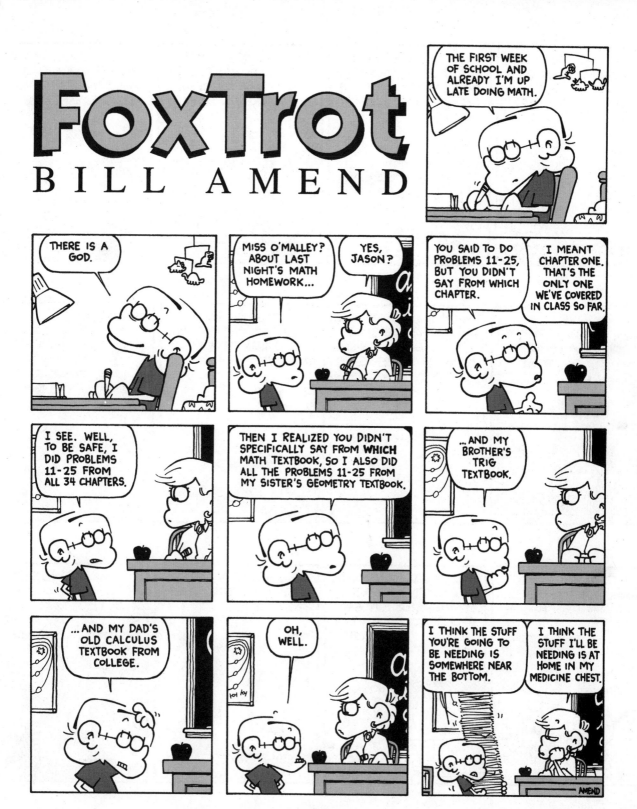

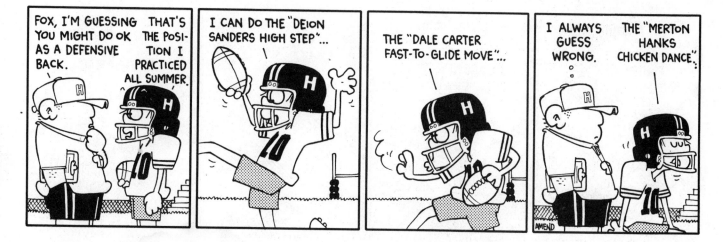

59

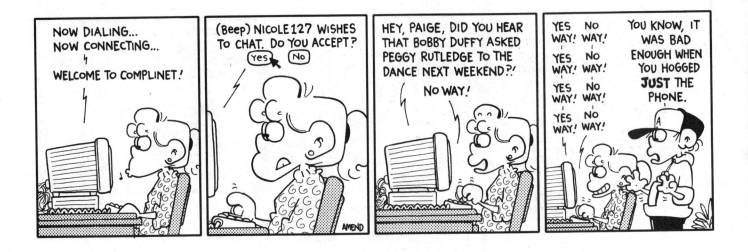

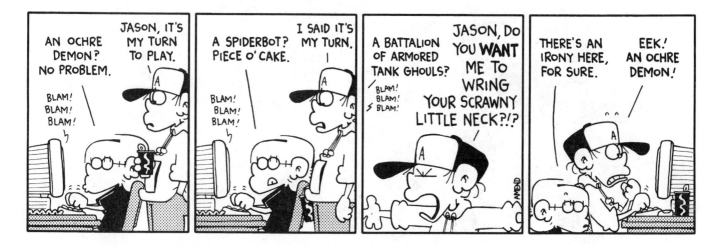

69

Jason's Challenge

Can you arrange these 12 pieces so that the dragon's fire forms one continuous loop?

Connect pieces by matching a white symbol to a black one of the same shape.

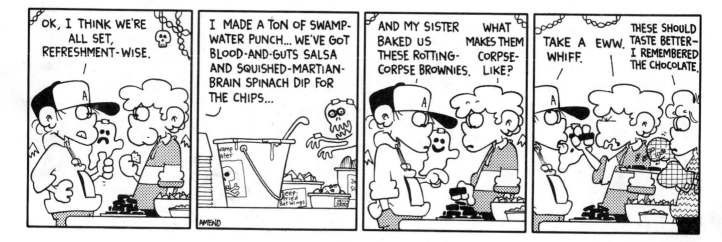

73

FoxTrot

BILL AMEND

FoxTrot
BILL AMEND

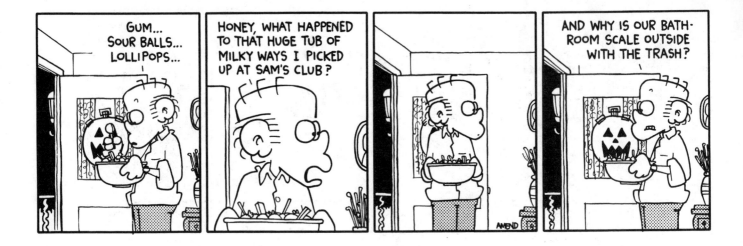

FoxTrot
BILL AMEND

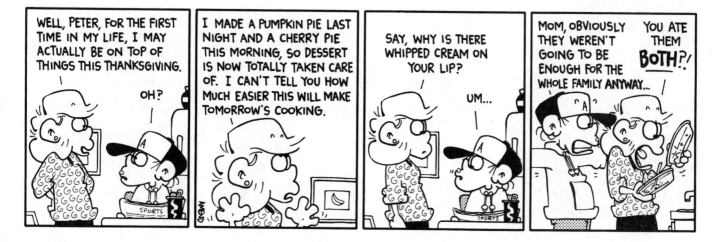

FoxTrot
BILL AMEND

99

FoxTrot
BILL AMEND

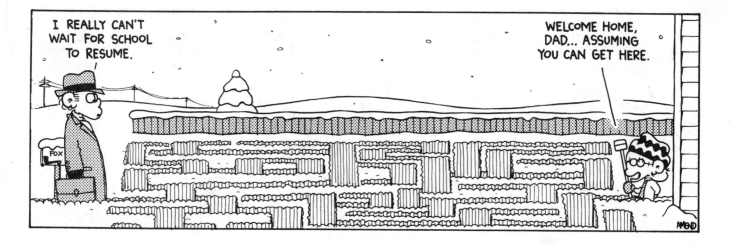

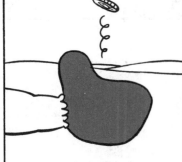

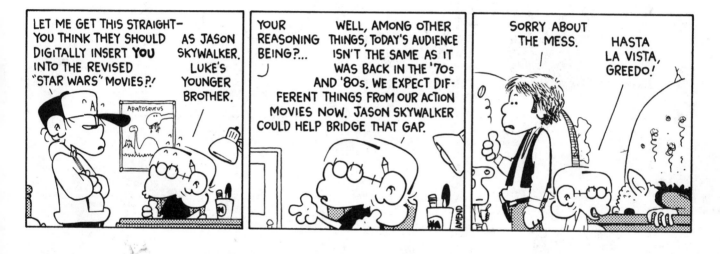

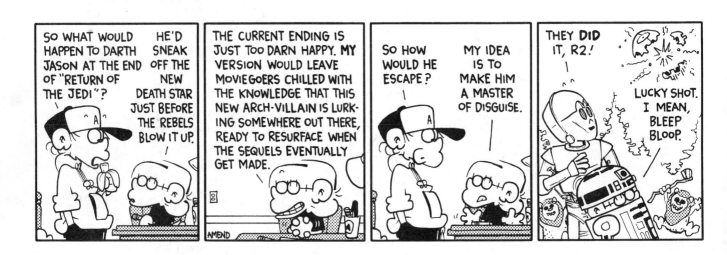

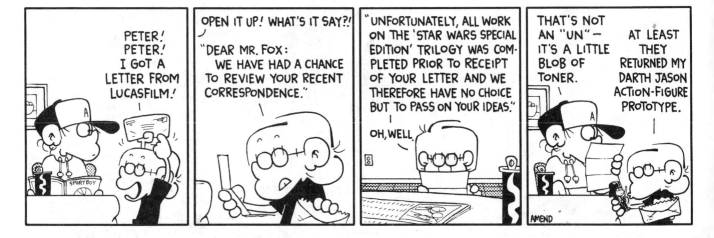

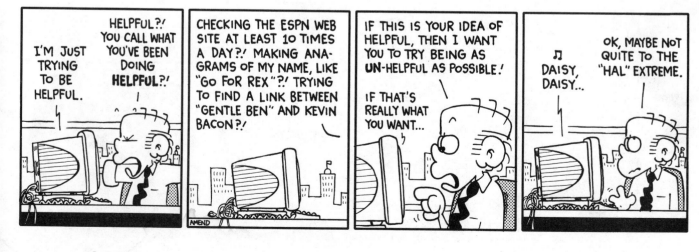

117

FoxTrot
BILL AMEND

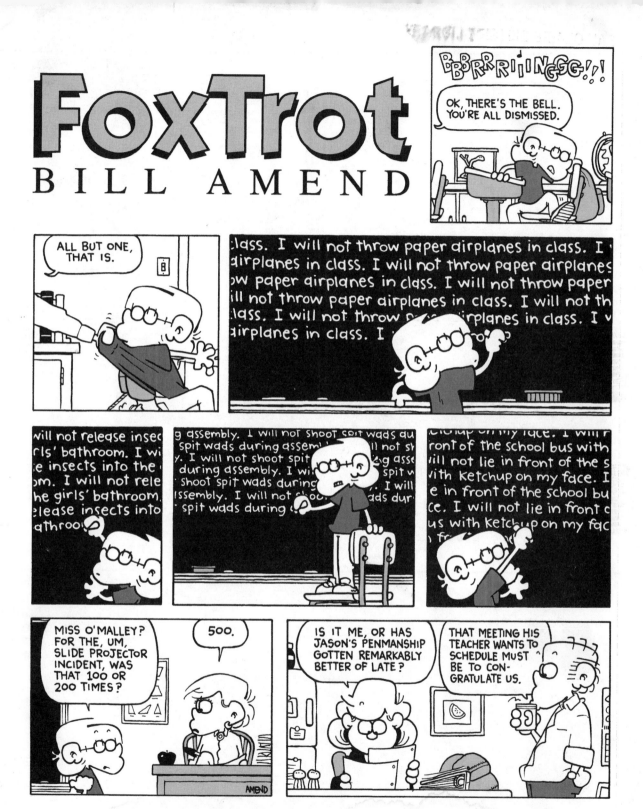